The Educator's Behavorial Guide

Tips for Every Teacher

Alana Simpson

The Educator's Behavorial Guide

© 2025 Alana Simpson. All rights reserved.
No part of this book may be reproduced, distributed, or otherwise used without prior written permission except as provided under fair use.

Dedication

I'm dedicating this book to my mom Janis, dad Clayton, and grandmothers, Denny and Hattie. These four people shaped me into the person I am today. They have been my greatest teachers; they taught me everything I know…never give up even in the face of adversity and the value of perseverance. They instilled in me the values of protecting my

family and extending a helping hand to others in need. I thought of them as I always do as I wrote this book; when times get tough keep on pushing through. Creating this book is a great accomplishment, and I hope I made them proud. I want to thank my Uncle

Walter (affectionately known as Jun) and my cousin Patrice for inspiring me and pushing me to do more. You believed in my potential and knew I could achieve anything I set my mind to. Your encouragement to never settle for the bare minimum and reach for the stars means the world to me. To Jackie, Carla, and Clayton - thank you for always being

there for me when I needed your support. To Catrell, Jayln, and Cali'Raye, my nephew and nieces, you fill my heart with endless joy and laughter. May you always chase your

dreams, embrace your curiosity, and find magic in every moment. You have been a

constant source of strength, love, and inspiration. This is for you with all my love and belief in the incredible future ahead of you. Family is the most precious thing, and I'm so grateful to have the best family anyone could ask for.

Acknowledgment

I want to say thank you to the ladies of LOD (right siders). I don't know what I would do

without you. We've been friends for 20 years, and we still have each other's backs. I'm so grateful for all your help in getting me to where I am with my books. Your continued love and support mean the world to me. Your unwavering support and love pushes to do

more. To all those who believe in the power of words to heal, inspire, and connect us. Thanks to Katrina Watters who is always there helping me when I need her support and guidance. To my TSDC friends who turned into family, I couldn't make it through the day without you. I want to send a thank you to my cousin Stephaine Parham for your support and help through this process.

Foreword

Behavior is communication.

I was a primary grade general education classroom teacher for twelve years before my middle son was diagnosed with severe nonverbal autism at the age of two. Before this, I had completed a rigorous teacher preparation program, hours of professional development, and earned a master's degree in interdisciplinary education. While I knew behavior is how children react to the world, I didn't really feel the mantra "behavior is communication" deeply until I had a child who could not speak to express his needs and emotions.

I was not only his mother in those early years of autism but often expected to wear the hats of therapist and teacher. I did my best, but the truth is what he taught me outweighed (and continues to outweigh) what I taught him. I am a more effective teacher because of my (now fifteen-year-old) son because I have become practiced at understanding and responding to student behavior.

Flipping the narrative from "This student is such a handful!" to "What is my student telling me with their behavior and how can I help?" will transform your relationships, enjoyment of your job, and efficacy as an educator.

My beautiful friend Alana Simpson has been an invaluable support to me as an autism mom and a general education teacher; I think you will also find her straightforward advice invaluable through this guide.

-Katrina Watters January 2025

Table of Contents

Welcome to the Classroom: Creating a Calm and Effective Classroom............1

Cracking the Code: Decoding Behaviors 4

Uncovering the Why: Identifying Triggers 8

The Power of Priming and Modifying 16

Finding Calm: Strategies to Ease Tension 24

Mastering Classroom Transitions..34

Calm in the Chaos: De-escalation Strategies for the classroom 39

Positive Pathways: Techniques for Redirecting Students Toward Success 43

The Power of Planned Ignoring...46

Building Success: The Power of Reinforcements..48

Prioritizing Self-Care in the Face of Behavioral Challenges 53

True Trigger Tales: Anecdotes from Ms. Alana 57

Conclusion: The Final Steps to Behavioral Success 61

Resources 64

Welcome to the Classroom: Creating a Calm and Effective Classroom

Your every day as an educator presents new challenges, opportunities, and students to engage with. Welcome to a resource designed with you in mind!

Managing behaviors in the classroom can feel like balancing on a tightrope—striving to meet academic goals while supporting the students' emotional and social needs. This book will guide you with proven strategies to create a positive, inclusive environment where students thrive. Whether you're a seasoned educator or just beginning, the tools within these pages will empower you to address challenging behaviors with confidence, compassion, and effectiveness.

Transitions are one of the most common sources of disruption in classrooms. Whether it's moving from one subject to another, lining up for lunch, or wrapping up an activity, transitions can overwhelm many students. I'll provide strategies to make these moments smooth and predictable, reducing stress for you and your class. You'll learn how to prepare students for what's coming next and help them shift gears with minimal resistance.

De-escalation is a critical skill for handling moments when emotions run high. Instead of reacting to a child's behavior, you'll learn to respond in ways that diffuse tension and prevent escalation. I'll give you practical examples to show you how to recognize early signs of distress and intervene before a full-blown meltdown occurs. These strategies will help individual students while maintaining a sense of safety and calm for the entire classroom.

Priming is a proactive approach to setting students up for success.

Priming gives students a preview of what to expect, helping them feel more prepared and less anxious. This is especially helpful for students who struggle with change or uncertainty. I will show you ways to incorporate priming into your daily routine, from previewing new activities to breaking down complex tasks into manageable steps.

Collaboration is another key component of effective behavior management. Throughout this book, I'll emphasize the importance of working with colleagues, parents, and support staff to create a consistent and supportive environment for your students. You'll learn how to build strong partnerships with families and leverage the expertise of your school's team to address challenging behaviors. Together, you can create a network of support that benefits every child.

In addition to these core topics, I'll discuss strategies for fostering connections in the classroom. Positive relationships are at the heart of good classroom management. When students feel seen, heard, and valued, they are more likely to engage positively. I'll share simple but powerful ways to build trust and rapport with your students, creating a foundation for learning and growth.

This book also focuses on the power of prevention. Many behavior challenges can be avoided with thoughtful planning and proactive strategies. I'll guide you through techniques for creating a structured, predictable environment that meets the diverse needs of your students. You'll learn how to set clear expectations, provide consistent consequences, and create a classroom culture that encourages positive behavior.

You'll find real-life examples, step-by-step guides, and practical tips throughout this book that you can implement right away. My goal is to make these strategies as accessible and actionable as possible so you see immediate results in your classroom. You'll also find encouragement and support because managing behaviors can be challenging, but it's also one of the most rewarding aspects of teaching.

Students with behavior challenges may have an Individualized Education Program (IEP) and a Behavior Intervention Plan (BIP). Building a strong relationship with the school's behaviorist and behavioral therapist(s) is essential for effectively supporting these students. Collaboration with them provides valuable insights into the student's triggers, successful strategies, and specific approaches you should implement in your classroom. This teamwork ensures consistency across environments and provides the students with the support they need to succeed.

Finally, I will address the importance of your own self-care as an educator. You must prioritize your well-being because managing behaviors can take a toll. You'll learn strategies for staying calm and centered, even in the face of challenging situations. You'll be better equipped to care for your students by taking care of yourself.

Together, we'll cover the tools and techniques you need to create a classroom where all students feel safe, supported, and ready to learn. I hope this book becomes a trusted resource you turn to again and again. Let's begin the journey towards a calmer, more effective classroom—one strategy at a time.

Cracking the Code: Decoding Behaviors

This chapter covers the intricacies of understanding, shaping, and modifying behaviors. I will define behavior and its functions. This chapter also provides tools to decode behavior and implement effective interventions.

Behaviors may be verbal, nonverbal, conscious, or unconscious. Children exhibit different behavior in different situations for different reasons.

Behavior has four functions: *attention, escape/avoidance, access to tangibles,* and *automatic reinforcement.*

Attention:

Seeking attention from adults or peers with disruptive behaviors sounds like loud talking, interrupting conversations, and making noise. Respond with planned ignoring, which is withholding attention to the unwanted behavior. When the student displays desirable behavior, respond with positive attention.

Escape/Avoidance:

Escaping or avoiding an unpleasant task occurs when an unpleasant request is made. It looks like a refusal to work, stalling, and avoiding the area altogether. A student may be disruptive in class to avoid an assignment. Respond by modifying the workload and giving the student breaks and choices of when to complete the task.

Access to Tangible:

Obtaining access to a desired object or activity such as a toy, food, or electronic device, is so rewarding the child will do anything to get it. Respond by encouraging the use of words to gain access to the object instead of maladaptive behavior (like tantrums). If the student is nonverbal, use gestures and body language, encouraging simple, intentional gestures like pointing, nodding, or shaking their head to communicate their needs.

Automatic Reinforcement:

Repetitive behaviors like hand-flapping and rocking are sensory-seeking behaviors, also known as "stimming." They produce sensory comfort for the student; it may be hard to redirect these behaviors because they are self-soothing and provide comfort. Respond with strategies that contradict the behavior, such as giving a fidget to hold instead of hand-flapping if you find the behavior is inappropriate for the setting.

If the student's behavior is not disruptive to other classmates, it may be fine to let them continue. However, if their proximity or actions make other students uncomfortable, you can provide alternative options to create a calm and inclusive learning environment. These options might include inviting the student to use the calm corner, designating another comfortable space in the room, or offering quiet activities that meet their needs, ensuring all students feel secure and respected. The goal is to balance individual accommodations with the needs of the entire classroom.

When you hear a behavioral therapist talk about the ABCs, they are referring to Antecedents, Behavior, and Consequences.

- *Antecedent: what happened immediately before the child's behavior*

- *Behavior: anything observable and measurable; actions of an individual*

- *Consequence: reinforcing or punitive response depending on whether the goal is to increase or decrease the behavior*

The antecedent sets the stage for behavior; it includes environmental cues, social interactions, verbal instructions, and internal thoughts.

Understanding the antecedent provides clarity on what influenced behavior and helps identify the trigger. This is true for both desirable and maladaptive behavior. A modification strategy for antecedents may decrease the likelihood of a repeat. For example, if a student exhibits maladaptive behavior whenever it's time to clean up, modify the antecedent (the phrase "clean up") by saying, "I'll help you put your things away, and you move one item."

Tracking behavior can help you understand them. I made tracking sheets charting frequency, duration, and characteristics of behaviors. You are trained observers and don't even know it; you see and deal with behavior every day. You can now collect and track data with these sheets. I understand that tracking behaviors can be time-consuming and tedious, but it is an incredibly valuable tool for identifying what was happening before a behavior occurred. By understanding the trigger or pattern, you can develop strategies to address the root cause and work toward preventing the behavior from happening in the future.

Consequences strengthen or weaken the likelihood of repeated behavior depending on reinforcement or punishment. Reinforcement provides rewards for positive behavior so the child connects desired items with a desired behavior.

Finding the ABCs reveals patterns of underlying behavior functions. What happens before the behavior is key to figuring out what triggers the student.

Trigger is another way to say *antecedent*. It may be as simple as a loud noise or a schedule change. As teachers, these things seem simple to us but they are not simple to all students. I believe a big part of teacher training is shedding our own thoughts and taking the student's perspective. You can't always give in, but having a little empathy goes a long way. Identifying the trigger helps you understand the function of your child's behavior.

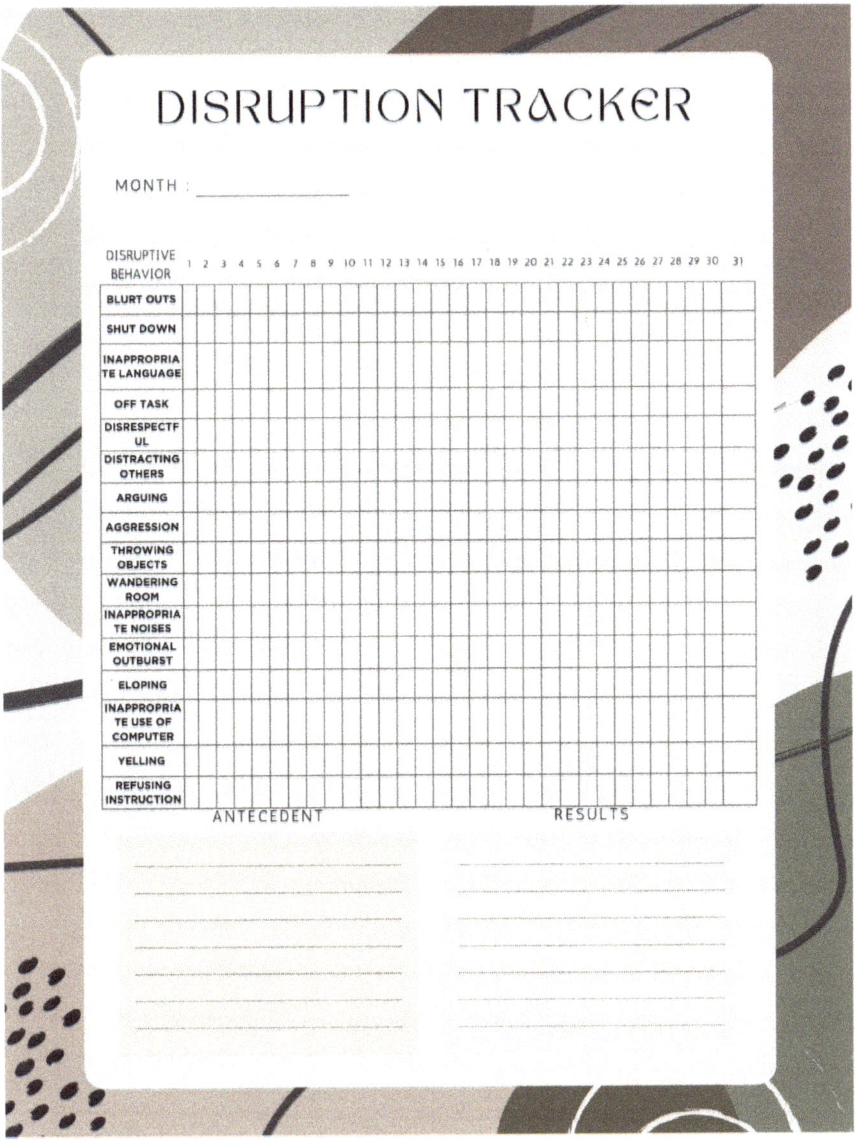

DISRUPTION TRACKER

MONTH : ____________

DISRUPTIVE BEHAVIOR	1	2	3	4	5	6	7	8	9	10	11	12	13	14	15	16	17	18	19	20	21	22	23	24	25	26	27	28	29	30	31
BLURT OUTS																															
SHUT DOWN																															
INAPPROPRIATE LANGUAGE																															
OFF TASK																															
DISRESPECTFUL																															
DISTRACTING OTHERS																															
ARGUING																															
AGGRESSION																															
THROWING OBJECTS																															
WANDERING ROOM																															
INAPPROPRIATE NOISES																															
EMOTIONAL OUTBURST																															
ELOPING																															
INAPPROPRIATE USE OF COMPUTER																															
YELLING																															
REFUSING INSTRUCTION																															

ANTECEDENT

RESULTS

Figure 1 Example of Disruption tracker

Uncovering the Why: Identifying Triggers

This chapter looks at triggers and explores how they shape our responses.

Learning a child's triggers increases your ability to head them off and prevent dysregulated behavior. You create a safe and supportive classroom environment. One of the most effective ways to do this is to understand triggers that may lead to challenging student behaviors.

Triggers are events, situations, or stimuli that provoke an emotional or behavioral response. These may vary widely among students; learning to identify and address them helps you maintain a positive learning environment. When teachers understand triggers, they can proactively intervene and reduce the likelihood of escalations while fostering student trust.

Common triggers include transitions, sensory overload, academic challenges, social dynamics' and sometimes even specific words or tones of voice triggers. For example, a student who struggles with change might become upset during unstructured or unpredictable moments, such as moving from one activity to another. Similarly, a child with sensory sensitivities might find loud noises or crowded spaces overwhelming, leading to behaviors like eloping, withdrawal, aggression, or frustration. Teachers can anticipate and minimize stressors when they proactively identify triggers, supporting students' emotional regulation.

Start with observation and documentation. Pay close attention to circumstances surrounding a student's challenging behaviors. Keep a journal or behavior log, noting what happened before, during, and after an incident.

Patterns will start to emerge, helping you identify potential triggers. For example, if a student consistently acts out during group work, this might indicate discomfort with social interactions or difficulty sharing materials.

Building relationships with students is another key strategy. The more you know about a child's background, preferences, and needs, the better equipped you'll be to recognize their triggers. Take time to have conversations with your students, learn about their interests and understand their unique personalities. When students feel seen and understood, they are more likely to communicate their needs verbally instead of through escalated behavior.

Priming is a proactive technique to help students navigate triggers. For example, if you know a student struggles with transitions, provide a heads-up before an activity change. Use a countdown timer, verbal reminders, or visual schedules to prepare them for what's next. Giving students adjustment time can reduce anxiety and improve their ability to transition smoothly. For instance, if you know you'll be absent and have a substitute, you may let the child know beforehand so they can process the change.

If you are a substitute teacher, you don't have the luxury of understanding student triggers and behaviors ahead of time. This guide provides you with tools to quickly assess, adapt, and address behaviors in real-time, helping you maintain control of the classroom while fostering respect and cooperation.

Recognize that your presence may disrupt usual classroom routines, which can be unsettling for some students, especially those who thrive on structure and consistency. Acknowledging goes a long way in building trust and reducing anxiety. You might say, "I know I'm not your regular teacher, and that can feel different. I'm here to help and make sure you have a good day. Let me know if you need a break or some extra support, and we'll figure it out together." Addressing the change openly and offering support creates a sense of safety and understanding. Additionally, allowing for breaks throughout the day gives children a way to self-regulate and manage their emotions, which helps maintain a positive learning environment for everyone.

Teaching self-regulation skills is another powerful tool. Help students recognize their own triggers and learn strategies to manage their emotions. For instance, teach deep breathing exercises, provide access to calming tools like stress balls and fidgets, or create a calming corner where students can take a break when they feel overwhelmed. These techniques support students at the moment and build lifelong skills for emotional regulation.

Collaborating with families and school staff provides insight into student triggers. Parents and caregivers understand what upsets or soothes their children. Similarly, working with special education teachers, behavioral therapists, psychologists, occupational therapists, and counselors helps develop a comprehensive plan to support students. This teamwork ensures consistency across home and school environments.

Flexibility in teaching approaches is critical. If a particular teaching style or classroom setup triggers a student, consider adjusting. For example, if a student becomes agitated during group activities, provide alternative options such as working with one partner instead of a group or changing the work setting from inside the classroom to outside. Small changes in seating arrangements, lighting, or noise levels can make a big difference.

Model calm and positive behavior. Students often mirror the emotions of adults around them. If you remain calm and composed during challenging moments, you create a sense of stability that helps students feel safe. Use a calm tone of voice, open body language, and empathic responses to de-escalate situations.

Identifying and addressing triggers is an ongoing process. As students grow and change, their triggers may evolve. Continuously reflect on your practices, seek feedback, and remain open to learning. By prioritizing the well-being of your students and equipping them with tools to manage their emotions, you create a classroom environment where all students can succeed.

Common Triggers:

- Loud noises
- Bright lights
- Strong smells
- Crowded environment
- Hunger
- Lack of sleep
- Physical illness
- Academics
- Transitioning between activities
- Temperature
- Clothing texture
- Cognitive overload
- Peer conflict
- Fire alarm
- Substitute teachers

Medication can affect behavior in both positive and negative ways. Many medications have side effects that may impact behavior. Overall, medications can be valuable in managing maladaptive behavior once you find the right dosage. If you suspect medication might be a trigger for a child's behavior and you have a strong rapport with the parents, you can provide them with a medication tracker as a resource. It's important to note I'm not suggesting you track the medication yourself. Instead, be aware medication changes or side effects are common triggers and can significantly impact behaviors.

Noise and light can be triggers. Noises like fire alarms or playgrounds are common triggers at school. A student may feel overwhelmed by loud sounds and try to elope. If a child is overwhelmed by playground noise you can work with support staff and try an alternative recess. The child still has playtime in a different area.

Fire alarms and drills can be overwhelming, especially for children who are sensitive to sudden loud noises or disruptions in routine. If you know a drill is scheduled, prime the child ahead of time to reduce anxiety and prevent potential behavioral challenges. Explain what will happen, why it's necessary, and how they can cope during the event. For example, you might say, "Today, there will be a fire drill. The alarm will be loud, but it's just practices to keep everyone safe. We'll walk outside together, and then we'll come back in when it's over." Use visuals, social stories, or role-playing to help the child understand the process. Have noise canceling headphones accessible, and talk to school support staff to see if offering the option of moving away from sounding bells is possible. When the child knows what to expect and feels supported, they're less likely to become overwhelmed, making the drill a smoother experience for everyone involved.

Children with light sensitivity may benefit from transition glasses that help when entering different rooms. Light coverings can be purchased to dim lights in the classroom. Pack a bag with headphones, earplugs, and sunglasses and leave them in an easily accessible place so you always have them when needed.

Schedules can be a trigger, leading to outbursts. Making a visual schedule will help the child know what to expect throughout the day. You can make a picture schedule or write it down.

Here are a few examples of trigger trackers you can use. You can also create your own using a program like Canva. Place a checkmark in the box on the date the trigger occurs so you can accurately track what triggers happen and when they take place. I've provided two different examples of trigger trackers for you to use. You can choose the one that best fits your time constraints and observation style, allowing you to effectively gather the most useful information.

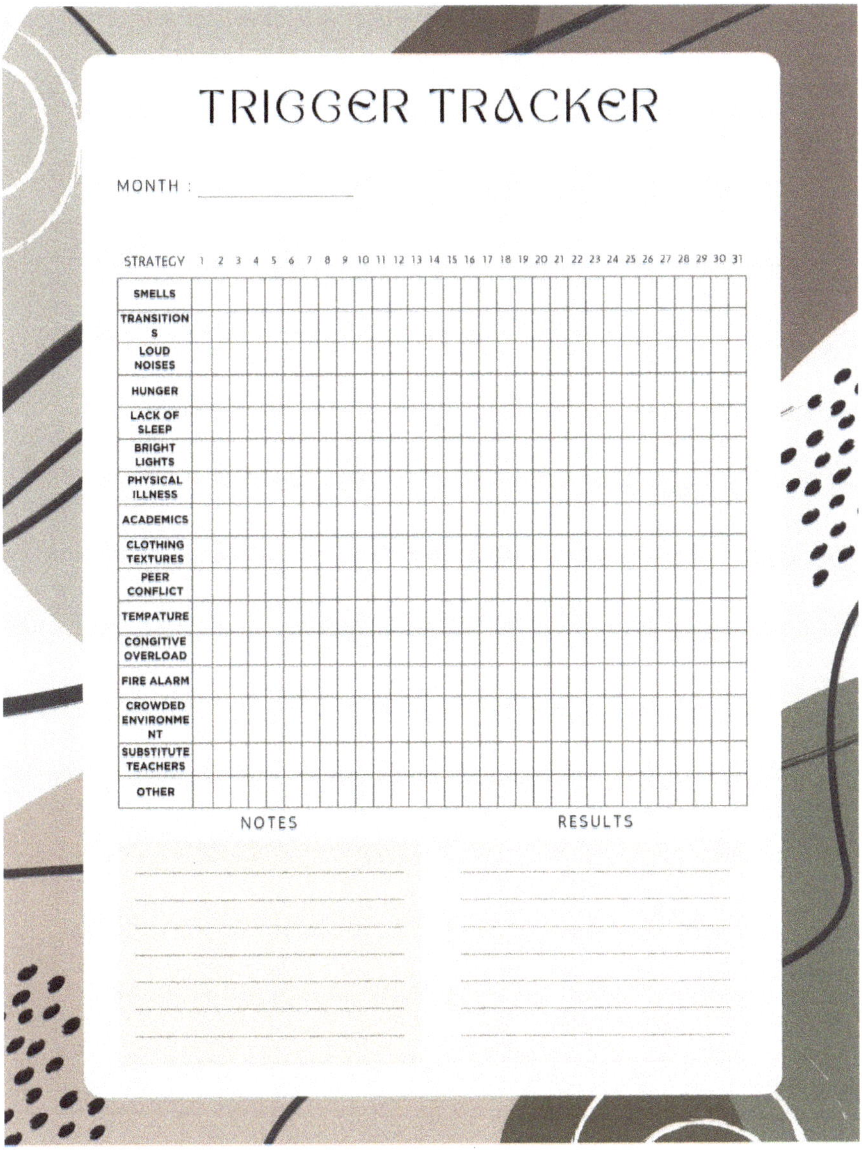

Figure 2 Example of Trigger tracker

TRIGGER TRACKER

| Date: | Start Time: | Finish Time: |

| Duration: | Location: |

Possible Triggers:
Loud noises   Bright lights   Strong smells   Crowded environment   Hunger
Lack of sleep   Physical illness   Academics   Transitioning between activities
Temperature   Clothing texture   Cognitive overload   Peer conflict   Fire alarm
Substitute teachers

If not here add it:

What subject was going:

What actions were taken:

What Happened:

Strategies used:

Figure 3 Example of Second Trigger tracker

MEDICATION LOG

NAME: _____   DATE: _____

#	MEDICATION / SUPPLEMENT	DOSE	DIRECTIONS	SIDE EFFECTS
1				
2				
3				
4				
5				
6				
7				
8				
9				
10				
11				
12				
13				
14				
15				
16				
17				
18				
19				
20				

Figure 4 Example of medication tracker

The Power of Priming and Modifying

Priming should be considered the first line of defense against maladaptive behavior. Priming sets children up for success by preparing them for what is about to happen. Priming's goal is to prepare children, so they know what to expect, which in turn lessens maladaptive behavior. Some children find comfort in routine and are rigid if the schedule is changed without notice. Another way to prime a child is by saying, "The iPad will turn off in two minutes." This indicates the time is about to end, so it is not a surprise when it turns off.

Priming is especially useful during events that deviate from the regular routine, such as field trips, guest speakers, or school assemblies. Teachers can prepare students by explaining the events in detail, addressing potential concerns, and outlining behavior expectations. For instance, before a field trip to a museum, review the schedule, describe what students will see, and discuss appropriate behavior, such as using indoor voices and staying with the group.

Incorporate priming by using countdown timers or verbal reminders during transitions. For example, say, "In five minutes, we'll clean up and move on to art class", followed by a reminder when there are two minutes remaining. These cues give students time to complete their current task and mentally prepare for the next one. Over time, these consistent practices build routines that help students feel more in control.

Priming is effective when introducing new or unfamiliar activities. For instance, before starting a science experiment, you might explain the steps involved, highlight key materials, and demonstrate the process. This helps students understand expectations and reduces confusion. For students who need additional support, you can provide individual priming sessions, offering one-to-one explanations or demonstrations before the group activity begins.

Visual schedules are excellent priming tools, especially for younger students or those with special needs. Visual schedules provide clear, step-by-step outlines of a day's activities, allowing students to anticipate what's next. For example, the teacher might display a schedule on the board that includes pictures or symbols for each subject or activity. Refer to the schedule throughout the day to reinforce predictability and reduce anxiety about changes.

If a child in your class has special activities throughout the day (like a speech or social skills session), collaborate with the support team to make a personal schedule for the desk. The student has access to the schedule and can add to or change the schedule. See below for a few examples of schedules you could use or create your own using tools like Canva. I've found the most effective schedules for students are laminated and designed with Velcro for easy adjustments. Laminating the paper ensures durability, preventing it from damage during daily use. Velcro allows you to quickly change subjects or activities as needed. Store subject icons in a pouch or box so they're accessible for the student. This setup ensures the schedule remains practical, flexible, and long-lasting.

Figure 5 Example of Weekly Schedule tracker

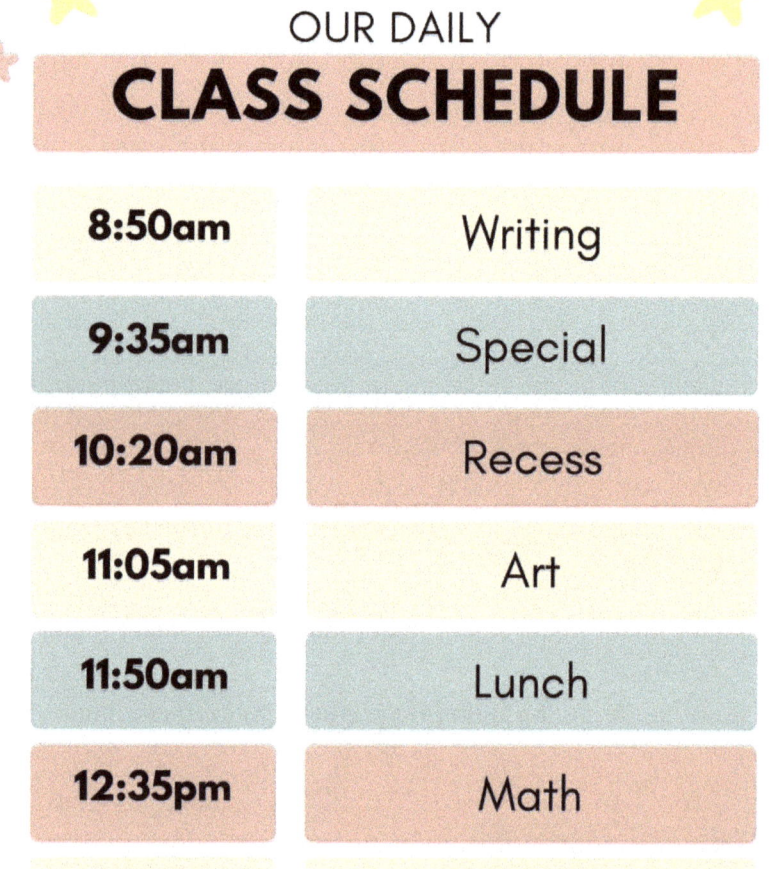

Figure 6 Example of Daily Schedule

Priming allows students to mentally and emotionally prepare for what's coming next. For example, a student who struggles with transitioning from recess to math may benefit from a five-minute warning and a brief explanation of the next activity. This gives the student time to shift gears and adjust their mindset, reducing resistance or disruptive behavior.

Priming can support social interaction. Teachers can prepare students for group activities by explaining roles, goals, and what effective collaboration looks and sounds like. For example, before a group project, you might assign roles like note-taker or presenter and review teamwork expectations. Describe each person's role, including what they are expected to do. This helps students understand their responsibilities and fosters confidence in participating.

Incorporating priming into daily routines creates a classroom environment that is predictable, supportive, and inclusive. Priming reduces anxiety and behavioral challenges while empowering students to approach tasks with confidence and clarity, setting them up for success in both academic and social settings.

If priming doesn't work, you can modify a request or task. Modifying the task means breaking it into smaller, more manageable steps. Focusing on one step instead of the entire task may ease frustration. Simplifying and breaking down instructions helps a child's understanding. For instance, if writing is a non-preferred task, offer to scribe while they tell you what to write. The work is completed with a bit of modification.

When discerning where modification is needed, identify the specific task requiring assistance and think about where you can maximize success and promote skill development. For example, if a worksheet's content is too large for a student to complete in one sitting, try doing the odd-numbered problems the first day and even-numbered ones the next day. Giving the student choice and input provides a sense of control. As teachers, you can change the wording of a request. Most children dislike the phrase "clean up. "Change it to "let's put these things away" or "I can help you pick up your things" and push the toys towards the child.

Demonstrate the task's steps and ask the child to observe what you do.

Modeling helps children understand expectations. Prompting and fading, such as verbal cues, gestures, and physical guidance, may be used to provide support and guidance. Slowly fade out prompts as the child becomes more independent.

The first/then strategy is another effective technique. Start by completing a less preferred task, then offer a more preferred task. Identify the task, determine what needs to be done, and then figure out the sequence. For instance, <u>first</u> reading is completed, <u>then</u> there is a break. Offer choices whenever possible; students may choose whether they want to read or do math first before they get a break. Kids love to voice their opinions, so give choices whenever possible.

Steps to make a first/then board:

- Prepare a board. You can find free templates on Canva.
- Draw the first/ then sections and laminate the page
- Attach Velcro dots
- Select pictures or symbols you want to use. Print, laminate, and Velcro them.
- Update as needed

Figure 7 Example of First/Then Board

PRIMING STRATEGIES

establish a routine	use visual supports
use timers	break tasks into smaller steps
relaxation techniques	calm and self-regulation techniques
social stories	choices
positive reinforcement	muscle relaxation
environmental modifications	breathing exercises
praise	sensory accommodations
first/then strategies	provide supportive guidance
offer breaks	be consistent
model expected behavior	use positive language to frame the task
make it fun	set clear expectations

Figure 8 Priming Strategies examples

Prevention is of paramount importance. After observing a student, identifying triggers and the function of behavior, you can implement prevention strategies. Utilizing strategies and subsequently monitoring their efficacy will be a great asset to you in preventing maladaptive behavior.

Below is a monthly tracker featuring various strategies to assist with this goal. Simply check off the strategy you've tried and note the result. Add any necessary notes. Using multiple strategies simultaneously may be the most effective approach. For example, providing a snack break with a timer, informing the student when time is nearly up, and communicating upcoming activities on the schedule.

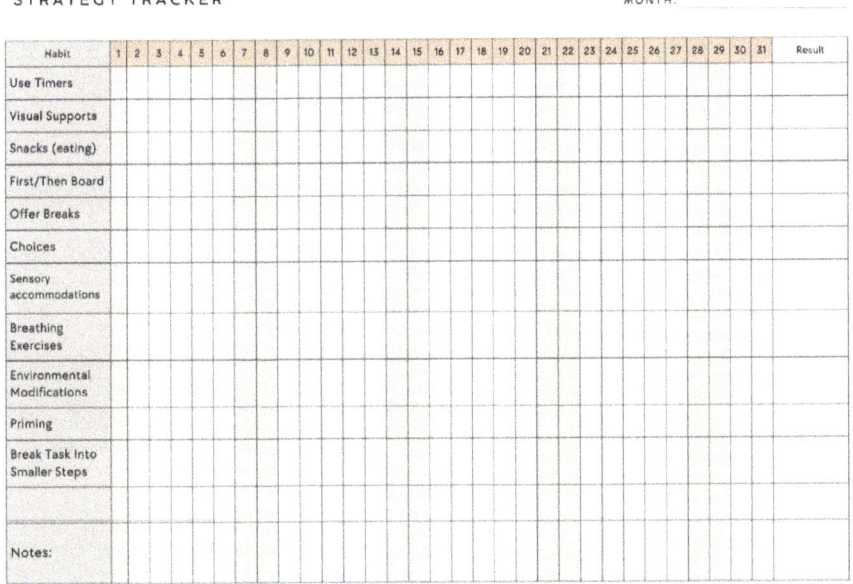

Figure 9 Example Strategy Tracker

Finding Calm:
Strategies to Ease Tension

We employ various strategies in ABA (Applied Behavioral Analysis) therapy to help children regulate emotions. Some teachers may feel a child is a "little off" or "not their usual self." This is *dysregulation*, a disruption in behavioral equilibrium that leads to unwanted, maladaptive behaviors. It may manifest in several ways, such as impulsivity, difficulty managing emotions, and anxiety. Behavior can range from an angry outburst to self-harm. Children may have mood swings and irritability that impact them daily. As with everything, everyone is different, so dysregulation will look unique to each student. Utilizing calming strategies may help regain control, effectively manage dysregulation, and enhance children's health.

Here are a few ways to teach skills that help regulate emotions and behavior while creating a supportive environment:

- <u>Establish routines</u>: Regular meal times and a daily schedule provide structure and consistency.

- <u>Teach emotional awareness</u>: Work with students to help them understand their emotions and discuss those emotions with them. Teach them it is okay to express emotions and validate their feelings.

- <u>Practice mindfulness</u>: Teach calming techniques like deep breathing exercises, coloring, meditation, and help them become aware of their thoughts.

- <u>Encourage self-regulation</u>: Teach calming strategies like counting to ten and positive self-talk.

- <u>Provide a safe space</u>: Create a space in your class where students can go to calm down when dysregulated. You may call it the "calm corner" or "cozy corner." Include pillows, a weighted blanket, and preferred items.

- <u>Model healthy coping skills</u>: You are a role model for desired behavior by managing your own emotions in a healthy way. Demonstrate problem-solving skills and empathy in your own life.

- <u>Positive reinforcement</u>: Reward the student when you notice positive behavior. Praise the child for using self-regulating skills.

Every student responds differently to strategies, so it may be challenging to find what works best. Don't become discouraged if it takes some trial and error to find what works!

Creating a sensory calming corner provides a safe, soothing place for a child to self-regulate. Work together to choose a retreat space when they need a break or feel overwhelmed. Decorate it with sensory-friendly materials like a bean bag, weighted blanket, and pillows. Add sensory tools like fidgets, stress balls, music, or textured items like a small sandbox. Some children like coloring books or reading books for relaxation. Create visual cues like break cards that signal the need for a calming break and do regular check-ins to see if breaks are needed. An example of a check-in would be saying, "Hey, little buddy, would you like a three-minute break or a five minute break?" Show the cards and have the child pick one. The following pages have examples of break cards and what typically goes in a calming corner. I've found five minute breaks work best. If the child needs more time, add one minute at a time and go from there.

Next, we will explore some tips and strategies designed to help with behavior management. Some students are nonverbal, others may struggle with speech, and some may shut down completely and not want to talk at all. It's essential to develop alternative ways to communicate with these students to ensure their needs are met and to foster meaningful connections. Functional communication refers to teaching students how to effectively communicate needs, wants, and feelings in a socially acceptable way. Many behavioral challenges in the classroom stem from a lack of communication skills; students may resort to crying, yelling or other disruptive behaviors when they cannot express themselves through language. Teaching functional communication equips students to appropriately interact with others and meet their needs without engaging in problematic behaviors.

Teaching functional communication is crucial for fostering independence and reducing frustration in students. For example, a student who struggles to verbalize needing help with a task might shut down. For example, when a student shuts down, you can check in by asking, "Do you need more time? And offer a simple choice thumbs up or thumbs down. If they give you a thumbs up, you can respond by saying, "Okay, I'll set a timer and check back with you when it goes off." You might have a disruptive student who is frustrated by a task that is presented to them, and they are being disruptive. By introducing simple and accessible communication methods like break cards, teachers help students effectively express themselves, leading to a calmer and more productive classroom environment. A student can easily access the card and give it to the teacher, signaling they need time apart from the class. This approach benefits individual students and enhances the entire class' overall learning experience.

Figure 10 Example Calm Corner

One example of functional communication in the classroom is teaching students to use visual supports like picture cards or communication boards. For instance, a nonverbal student might use a card with an image of a bathroom to signal they need to leave the room. Similarly, communication boards with icons for common requests- such as "help" or "finished"- empowers students to convey their needs quickly and clearly. These tools are especially helpful for students with autism, apraxia, and other communication challenges. Here are some other forms of communication that many people may not consider, but they are highly effective, and ones used every day with our kids.

1) Written Communication: Whiteboards, letter boards, and notebooks

2) Gestures: Encouraging pointing, nodding, or shaking their heads

3) Partner-Assisted Communication: The teacher points to an object, and the student indicates their choice by looking at the object

4) Emotion Charts: A visual tool to help students indicate how they are feeling.

5) Behavioral Communication: The student is pulling towards what they want or need. I have seen this when the student is too embarrassed to tell you what they want or need.

These forms of communication are really tailored to fit the student's individual strengths, preferences, and development levels. Collaboration with speech, the behaviorist, and other specialists at the school can further help you with which of these forms of communication works best for the student.

Figure 11: Communication Card

For verbal students who may need help refining communication skills, teachers can model and encourage specific phrases. For example, teach a student to say, "Can you help me?" instead of acting out when they are stuck on a task. Role-playing activities are also effective, allowing students to practice using functional phrases in a low-pressure setting. For instance, you might rehearse scenarios where the student politely asks for a turn or expresses a need for a break.

The key to successful functional communication is consistency and practice. Embed communication opportunities into daily routines by prompting students to use words, visual supports, or devices before fulfilling requests. For example, prompt a student to use a picture card or verbalize "I want crackers" before giving a student a snack. Over time, students learn to associate communication with having their needs met, subsequently reinforcing positive behavior and reducing frustration. By prioritizing functional communication in the classroom, teachers create a supportive environment for all learners.

Figure 12: Example of Calm Corner

Figure 13: Calming Strategies

Figure 14 Calm Down Chart

CALMING STRATEGIES

weighted blankets	create a calm corner
fidgets	music
blow bubbles	take a break (have a snack, read, be alone)
yell into a pillow	rip paper or boxes
break popsicle sticks	go for a walk
pressure massage (head, arms, legs)	headphones, earplugs
give space (set a timer and check-in)	drawing
deep breathing	drink water
make a fort	squeeze playdough or clay
chewing gum	kinetic sand
play with slime	run a lap
Legos	stress ball

Figure 15 Calming Strategies Examples

Mastering Classroom Transitions

Transitions are defined as moving from one activity to another. These can be difficult for many students, especially those who thrive on routine or struggle with change. Unclear expectations, abrupt shifts, or lack of structure can lead to confusion, frustration, or behavioral challenges. Transitions may mean leaving behind something enjoyable or facing a less engaging or stressful activity for some students. Recognizing these challenges is the first step in managing transitions effectively.

Providing clear cues and signals helps students anticipate and prepare for transitions. Visual timers, verbal warnings, or nonverbal signals like clapping patterns or flicking the lights alerts students a change is coming. For example, saying, "We'll clean up in five minutes and move to our next activity," gives students time to prepare. Repeating instructions and using consistent signals ensures students understand what's expected, reducing uncertainty.

Effective transition strategies include creating routines, using visuals, and breaking tasks into manageable steps. For instance, using a picture schedule helps younger students or those with special needs understand the sequence of activities. Pairing a countdown with positive reinforcement, such as praising students for transitioning quickly and quietly, motivates them to follow the routine. Additionally, engaging students in transition-related tasks, like being a line leader or helping clean up, provides a sense of ownership and focus.

Students transition at different paces, so it's important to be flexible and provide individualized support. Some may need additional prompts, while others might benefit from a transitional object, such as holding a sensory item to ease the process. If a student struggles, take a moment to acknowledge their feelings and offer guidance, such as, "I see it's hard to stop what you're doing, but we can come back to this later." Building in a few extra moments for those who need it ensures smoother transitions for everyone while maintaining a calm and supportive classroom environment.

Sometimes, it takes a sense of humor and trying something unexpected to help a student transition. Once, I was working with a student who didn't want to go from one classroom to the next, so I turned it into a fun competition. I looked at the student and said, " I bet I'm faster than you!" and took off running. The student immediately followed, trying their best to beat me to the classroom. As I approached the door, I slowed down just enough to let the student win, knowing losing was a trigger for demand and could cause another behavior. When the students reached the classroom, they were happy and excited, believing they had won. They didn't realize I let them, but my objective was achieved: we had a successful transition to the next classroom, and they arrived in a positive and cooperative mood.

Strategies for Smooths Transitions

1. **Prepare in advance**

Why it works: Preparation reduces anxiety by creating predictability.

How to do it:

- Use visual schedules or a calendar.

- Give a clear heads-up: "In 5 minutes, we're going to clean up for the next subject."

- Use timers: set a 5-minute timer and say, "When the timer beeps, it's time to go".

Example: The student is watching a video. Instead of saying, "Turn it off now," say, "In 5 minutes, the video will end, and we'll start getting ready for your break to end". When 5 minutes are up, say, "It's time to turn it off. Let's get ready for the next subject".

2. **Provide Visual or Verbal Cues**

Why it works: Many students process visual or verbal information better than abstract instructions.

How to do it:

- Use pictures: Show an image of shoes when it's time to leave.
- Use first/then language: "First we clean up, Then we play outside."

Example: If transitioning from play to homework, use a visual chart showing a toy and a book. Say, "First, we finish homework, then you can play again."

3. **Offer Choices**

Why it works: Giving students a sense of control can reduce resistance. How to do it:

Present two options: "Do you want to write, or do you want to read the book?"

- Make it manageable: Avoid overwhelming them with too many choices.

Example: When transitioning to the next subject, you can say, "Do you want to write the sentences, or do you want me to scribe for you?"

3. **Set a Positive Tone**

Why it Works: A cheerful and engaging approach reduces power struggles. How to do it:

- Use upbeat language: "Let's see who can clean up the fastest!"
- Celebrate small successes: "Great job cleaning up and putting away your toys!"

Example: When transitioning to lunch, say, "Wow, I can already smell lunch! Let's race to the servery!"

4. **Acknowledge Feelings**

Why it works: Validating emotions helps children feel heard and reduces frustration.

How to do it:

- Acknowledge their feelings: "I know you're having fun, and it's hard to stop playing."
- Offer empathy: "I'd feel upset too if I had to stop something I enjoyed."

Example: The student doesn't want to come in from recess. Say, "I can see you're sad to come in. Let's set a timer for 1 more minute, and then you can come in."

5. Debrief Afterward

Why it works: Reviewing helps children learn and build confidence. How to do it:

- Talk about what went well: "You did great listening when it was time to line up!
- After a tough transition, say, "Today was hard, but we got through it. What could we try tomorrow to make it easier?"

Putting It All Together: A Sample Transition Routine Scenario: Transitioning from recess to class.

1. Prepare: "In 5 minutes, you'll come in from recess".
2. Cue: Set a timer or show a picture of the classroom.
3. Acknowledge: "I know it's hard to stop playing-it's so much fun!"
4. Choices: "Do you want 1 or 2 minutes to stay out?"
5. Positive tone: "Let's see who can get to class the fastest!"
6. Celebrate: You did it! Now it's time to go to class."

Final Thoughts

Transitions are opportunities for connections and growth. With preparation, empathy, and consistency, they can become smoother and less stressful for both teachers and students.

Calm in the Chaos: De-escalation Strategies for the classroom

De-escalating a situation begins with recognizing early warning signs of distress or agitation in students. These might include changes in tone of voice, body language, or increased fidgeting. As the teacher, remain observant and proactive when you notice these signals. Addressing behavior early with a calm and supportive approach can often prevent further escalation. Simple actions like making eye contact, acknowledging the student's feelings or redirecting their attention to a task help diffuse tension before it grows.

Your demeanor plays a critical role in de-escalation. Remaining calm and composed, even in the face of challenging behavior, sets the situation's tone.

Speak in a slow, steady tone and avoid raising your voice, which could further agitate the student. Use neutral language and avoid confrontational statements. For example, instead of saying, "Stop acting out," try", "I can see you're upset. How can I help you right now?" You convey empathy and show the students you're there to support, not punish them.

Sometimes, the best way to de-escalate a situation is to give the student space. When a student is upset or overwhelmed, it's important to give space to calm down before trying to engage in a conversation. Let the students know you understand they need a moment. Say, "I see you're upset. I'll give you five minutes to take a break, and I'll check back to see if you need more time or if you're ready to talk". You are showing the student you respect their need for space while also providing a clear timeline for follow-up.

Gently check back in with the student after the said time. Say something like, "How are you feeling now? Do you need a little more time, or would you like to talk about it?" This gives them options to let you know if they're ready to communicate or still need to self-regulate. It's important to remain calm and patient, allowing them to take the lead when they're ready to discuss what's going on.

This strategy helps the student feel supported and teaches them to self-regulate and communicate their needs. It prevents the situation from further escalation by avoiding pushing the students to talk before they're ready.

If possible, allow the student a moment away from the class to regroup.

Try a designated calm-down spot in the classroom or suggest a brief walk in the hallway. Let the student know it's okay to take a break and they can rejoin the class when they feel ready. This helps the student regulate their emotions and prevents the situation from disrupting the class.

Once the student calms down, help them transition back into the classroom routine.

Briefly review expectations and offer positive reinforcement for their effort to re-engage. For example, "Thank you for taking a moment to calm down. Let's get back to your work-I'm here to help if you need anything." This reinforces that challenges are a normal part of the day and can be addressed without judgement. You create an atmosphere of respect and accountability by maintaining consistency and support.

De-escalation Strategies To Remember Daily

1. **Control Your Own Emotions**

Take deep breaths, lower your voice, and use open body language. Remember: Students mirror your emotional state.

Example: If the student is yelling, respond with a calm, steady voice: "I hear you're really upset. I'm here to help."

2. **Validate Their Feelings**

Acknowledge what they're experiencing without judgment. Avoid dismissive phrases like "calm down" or "you're fine."

Example: "I see you're feeling really frustrated because you had to stop playing. That can be really hard".

3. Give Space, If Needed

Some students need physical or emotional space to self-regulate. Create a safe, quiet environment where they can decompress.

Example: "I'll set a five-minute timer and check in when it goes off. I'll be right here when you're ready to talk.

4. Use Visual or Verbal Cues

For younger or neurodivergent students, visual aids like emotion cards or calming charts can help.

Example: Show a picture of the "Breathe in, breathe out" steps while saying: "let's take a slow breath together. In and out.

5. Redirect to a Calming Activity

Offer activities that help self-soothe, like squeezing a stress ball, drawing, or listening to calming music.

Example: Would you like to color or play with a sensory toy to feel better?

6. Break Down the Problem

Help them identify the issue and work toward a solution once they're calmer.

Example: It sounds like you're upset because your brother took your toy. Let's figure out how to solve this problem together.

7. Practice Active Listening

Give them your full attention, maintain eye contact, and repeat what they're saying to show understanding.

Example: Student: "I don't want to stop playing on my IPad!"

Teacher: "You don't want to stop playing on your IPad because you're having fun. I understand" I can set a timer for five more minutes.

8. **Offer Choices**

Empower them with simple, controlled choices to regain a sense of control.

Example: "Do you want to read now or in five minutes?"

9. **Teach and Practice Calming Techniques**

Introduce strategies like deep breathing, progressive muscle relaxation, or mindfulness during calm moments so they're easier to use when needed.

Example: "Let's blow out imaginary candles together. Take a big breath in, and blow it out slowly."

Challenges and Solutions

1. **Student Doesn't Respond Immediately**

Solution: Stay patient and consistent. Sometimes, they need more time to calm down.

2. **Teacher Feels Overwhelmed**

Solution: Take a quick pause if possible. Model calming strategies for yourself.

3. **Meltdown Persists**

Solution: Focus on safety and use minimal interaction until they show signs of calming. Then, reintroduce strategies.

Positive Pathways: Techniques for Redirecting Students Toward Success

Student redirection is one of the most effective tools for managing classroom behavior. It allows you to guide students back to appropriate activities or behaviors without escalating a situation. Redirection shifts the student's focus from a disruptive, off-task behavior to a constructive alternative. Approaching redirection calmly and confidently maintains classroom order and helps students stay engaged without singling them out or causing embarrassment.

Language that redirects students influences the outcome. Instead of focusing on what is wrong, frame your direction in a positive way. For example, instead of saying, "Stop talking and pay attention," "Try," "Let's focus on the instructions so we can finish on time." This redirects behavior and reinforces the desired outcome. Positive language keeps the atmosphere respectful and reduces the likelihood of resistance.

Sometimes, the best way to redirect is to give the student a purposeful task or movement break. For instance, if a student is restless or disruptive, ask them to pass out materials, organize supplies, or assist with a small task. These activities can refocus energy in a productive way and give a sense of responsibility. Movement-based redirection is particularly effective for younger students or those who struggle sitting for long periods.

Use questions or choices to steer the student back on track. For example, ask a disengaged student, "Would you like to work on this part of the activity or start with something easier?" Providing choices offers control while still aligning their actions with classroom expectations. Questions encourage self-reflection, prompting students to think about their behavior and make adjustments on their own.

Once a student has been successfully redirected, it's important to acknowledge their effort. Positive reinforcement encourages more good choices. A simple statement like "Thank you for getting back on task so quickly" reinforces behavior and sets a positive tone for the rest of the lesson. Combining clear guidance with positive reinforcement creates an environment where students feel supported and are more likely to respond positively to future redirection.

I've found that when a student displays disruptive behavior, using a calm but stern voice to say, "No thank you", often stops the behavior immediately. If the student continues, I follow up with, "Try again," which usually prompts them to stop. Once they've adjusted their behavior, I reinforce their compliance by saying, "Great job listening," and then providing them clear directions on what I want them to do next. This approach sets firm boundaries while acknowledging and encouraging positive behavior, guiding the student toward the desired actions.

Types of Redirection

1. **Distraction-Based Redirection**: Diverts the student's attention to something more engaging or interesting.

Example: "Oh wow, look at this toy car! It's so fast. Want to race it with me?"

2. **Verbal Redirection:** Guides the student toward appropriate behavior with clear instructions.

Example: "Feet stay on the floor. If you want to jump, let's go outside and jump on the trampoline!"

3. **Choice-Based Redirection:** Offers two acceptable options to give the student a sense of control.

Example: "You can color with crayons or play with blocks. Which one would you like?"

4. **Calming Redirection:** Helps the student regulate their emotions by providing soothing alternatives.

Examples: "It seems like you're upset. Let's take some deep breaths together or sit with your sensory toy for a bit."

5. **Activity Redirection:** Channels energy into a constructive or meaningful activity.

Example: "Instead of climbing on the couch, how about we build a tower with these cushions?"

6. **Problem-Solving Redirection:** Encourages critical thinking and problem-solving skills.

Example: "We can't play with that right now. Can you think of something else we can do with these materials?"

Steps to Effectively Redirect

1. **Stay Calm and Present:** Your tone, body language, and words should convey calmness and patience.

2. **Identify the Triggers**: Understand the reason behind the behavior (boredom, sensory seeking, frustration)

3. **Acknowledge the Child's Feelings:** Validate their emotions before redirecting.

Example: "I see you're really excited to explore. Let's find a safe way to do that".

4. **Use Clear and Positive Language:** Focus on what the child can do, not what they shouldn't do.

5. **Offer an Immediate Alternative:** Provide an engaging, appropriate option that matches their needs.

6. **Follow Through with Encouragement:** Praise or reinforce their positive behavior after they transition.

Example: "Great choice! You're so creative with those blocks."

The Power of Planned Ignoring

Planned ignoring is a behavioral strategy where attention is withheld from specific, minor, and non-dangerous behaviors to avoid reinforcing them. It is rooted in the principle that attention, whether positive or negative, serves as a powerful reinforcer for behavior such as whining, interrupting, or making off-topic comments. Responding-even with reprimands- can unintentionally reinforce those actions. By intentionally ignoring these behaviors, a teacher can reduce their frequency over time.

This technique is effective for behaviors that do not harm or disrupt the entire class. For example, a student who loudly taps their pencil during a lecture might be seeking attention. If the teacher calls out the behavior, the student may feel rewarded even though it is negative attention. If the teacher remains focused on the lesson and refrains from reacting, the behavior is less likely to be reinforced and may decrease. Planned ignoring helps students understand attention is earned through positive actions rather than disruptive ones.

The effectiveness of planned ignoring lies in its strategic use alongside positive reinforcement. While ignoring unwanted behaviors, teachers should simultaneously acknowledge and praise appropriate behaviors. For instance, if one student is calling out answers while others are raising their hands, the teacher might ignore the disruption and instead say, "I really appreciate how Alex is raising his hand, waiting to be called on." This shifts the focus towards desirable behavior, encouraging the disruptive student to adjust their actions to gain recognition.

Consistency is crucial for planned ignoring to work. Teachers must avoid giving in to the behavior, even if it escalates temporarily- a phenomenon known as an *extinction burst*. During this phase, a student might intensify behavior to regain attention. However, if attention is withheld, the behavior will eventually decrease. Communicate you are using this strategy for certain behavior when support staff are in your classroom to ensure everyone responds consistently.

While planned ignoring can be highly effective, it is not appropriate for all situations. Teachers should never use planned ignoring in dangerous, harmful, or unsafe behaviors, as these require immediate interventions. Planned ignoring is most successful when part of a larger behavioral management plan, complemented by clear expectations, consistent consequences and positive reinforcements. When implemented correctly, it empowers you to reduce disruptions while fostering a classroom environment that prioritizes positive interactions and learning.

Building Success:
The Power of Reinforcements

Reinforcements shape behavior, actions, and decisions. Reinforcements can be as simple as verbal praise or as intricate as a reward store system. We will go through different rewards to find which is best for students. Conduct a preference assessment to determine what your students like and are motivated by. Avoid randomly selecting reinforcements and rewards; this approach may not effectively reduce maladaptive behavior.

You can decide if *intermittent* or *scheduled* reinforcement is most effective. Intermittent means randomly catching expected behavior and offering a reward. Scheduled means reinforcement is given every time for the desired behavior. Scheduled or intermittent reinforcements may lead to stronger and more persistent behavior if the child associates reward with expected behavior. The reward must be motivating to be effective.

You can implement a token board system. A token board is a visual tool used in behavioral management. It is usually a board with five spaces for tokens with tasks listed for the child to complete. It's particularly effective for students who need extra motivation or struggle with intrinsic rewards. The board typically includes five to ten spaces for tokens, which can be stars, smiley faces, or tokens, and a space to display the reward the student is working for.

Many people often overlook the importance of conducting preference assessments, assuming that students only want to have a break or a specific toy. However, preferences can change over time, and it's essential to periodically revisit and reassess what motivates a student to ensure the chosen reinforcers remain effective and meaningful.

Preference assessments are tools used to identify items, activities, or experiences that a child finds motivating or enjoyable. These assessments are particularly important for neurodivergent children, as they help caregivers and educators determine effective reinforcers for teaching new skills or encouraging desired behaviors. Preference assessments can take various forms, such as observing the child's natural choices, presenting a selection of items for them to pick from, or systematically evaluating how they interact with or respond to specific stimuli. By understanding a child's preferences, caregivers can create personalized strategies that promote engagement and make learning experiences more rewarding.

Introduce the token board to the student by explaining how it works in simple terms. For example, you might say: " This is your token board. Every time you follow directions, stay on task or raise your hand, you'll earn a token. Once you fill up all the spaces on your board, you can pick a reward from your list." Be sure to show them the possible rewards, which could include things like extra computer time, a small prize, or a preferred activity.

Token boards work best for specific, targeted behaviors. For instance, if a student struggles with staying seated during independent work time, use the token board to reinforce that behavior. Say, "Each time you stay in your seat for five minutes, I'll give you a token. Once you earn all five tokens, you can choose a reward!"

It's essential to deliver tokens immediately when the desired behavior occurs, along with specific praise such as, "Great job staying in your seat! Here's your token." This helps the student make a clear connection between their behavior and the reward. If the student struggles, provide gentle reminders and encouragement, such as, "Remember, we're working on earning tokens for staying in our seat."

By introducing the token board in a positive way, maintaining consistency, and ensuring the rewards are meaningful and distributed on time to the student, this tool can become a highly effective strategy for improving behavior and fostering a positive environment.

A reward store system reinforces desired behaviors through the exchange of points, tokens, stars, or money. Implement these steps before setting up your store:

- ☐ Tell the student what the expected tasks or behaviors are.
- ☐ Establish the token economy you will use.
  - Will you be using points, coins, stars, or fake money? WIll they be physical or digital?
  - Where will you keep track of the points earned? Will it be a physical or digital tracker?
  - Selecting reinforcement items for the store should be motivating.
- ☐ Set prices for items; make sure prices are reasonable and achievable.
- ☐ Establish rules for the store like when items can be purchased.
  - Rules should include guidelines for behavior expectations, token distribution, and consequences for rule violations.
- ☐ Be consistent with the upkeep of the store and the items.
- ☐ Track the effectiveness of the reward store system; make necessary adjustments.
- ☐ Provide feedback to the student. Praise positive behavior and award extra points or tokens for exceptional behavior. This is usually very motivating to a child and promotes positive behavior change.

The following provides step-by-step instructions for making a customized token board to help motivate and reinforce desired behavior.

- <u>Gather materials</u>: You will need to make a template on Canva or PowerPoint to create the board and the tokens.
- <u>Design the board</u>: Decide how you want the board to look. Do you want designs on the border or pictures? Add a title to the board.
- <u>Divide the board into sections</u>: Decide how many sections you want on the board - commonly five or ten are used. Each section represents a task to be completed.

- <u>Add reward cards</u>: What is the child working after completing the task? Laminate all materials that were made.

- <u>Attach velcro dots</u>: Attach velcro dots to the board and the backs of the tokens. Make sure there is enough space between each dot to easily attach and remove.

The following page has an example of a completed token board featuring tokens and reinforcement pieces.

Figure 16 Token Board Example

Once your token board is complete, proceed with the following steps:

- Introduce the token board: Explain the token system to the student and let them know each time they complete a task or demonstrate positive behavior, they earn a token to be placed on the board.

- Reward system: Determine the number of tokens needed to earn the reward. It can be a small reward, screen time, or a preferred activity.

- Celebrate success: Once the student has earned all the tokens, celebrate their success and provide the reward.

- Review and adjust: Regularly review if the token board is working and make adjustments as necessary to the task, rewards, or the layout of the board to better suit the child.

Prioritizing Self-Care in the Face of Behavioral Challenges

Teaching is a rewarding but demanding profession, and dealing with challenging behaviors in the classroom can take a significant emotional and mental toll on teachers. It's important to recognize when you're feeling overwhelmed and take proactive steps to address your well-being. Self-care isn't a luxury-it's essential for maintaining the energy and resilience needed to support students. Acknowledging the emotional challenges that come with teaching is the first step towards cultivating a sustainable and fulfilling career.

Seek support from colleagues and specialists when you're feeling stressed or uncertain about managing behaviors; don't hesitate to reach out to others for support. Talking to other teachers, the school behaviorist, or other staff who specialize in behavior management can provide valuable insight and practical coping and stress management strategies.

Engaging in regular reflection on your own practices and discussing experiences with colleagues can be incredibly therapeutic. Consider joining or forming a peer support group where teachers can openly share successes and struggles. This kind of environment fosters camaraderie and helps you realize you're not alone in your challenges. Hearing how others manage similar situations can inspire fresh approaches and remind you of your progress, even when it feels like an uphill battle.

Mindfulness practices such as deep breathing, meditation, or yoga are powerful tools for managing stress. Taking even a few minutes during the school day to practice controlled breathing can help you reset and approach difficult situations with a clear head. For example, if you've just had a particularly stressful interaction, stepping away for five deep breaths can help you regain composure before addressing the next challenge. These small moments of mindfulness positively influence your mental health over time.

Setting boundaries between work and personal life prevents burnout. Avoid bringing work-related stress home by establishing a clear end to your workday. For instance, set a rule to stop checking emails after a certain time in the evening or limit the amount of time you spend grading papers at home.

Instead, dedicate that time to activities that bring you joy and relaxation, whether it's spending time with loved ones, pursuing hobbies, or simply unwinding with a good book.

Some examples of self-care practices are physical activities like walking, running, or attending a fitness class. These release tension and improve your mood. Even a ten-minute stretch break during the day makes a difference.

Journaling -writing down your thoughts and feelings about your day- helps you process emotions and identify patterns of stress. Journaling also helps identify triggers that contribute to stress.

Connecting with others is self-care. Schedule time to meet with friends, family, or trusted colleagues to talk, laugh, and share. Social connections are vital for maintaining emotional balance. Engaging in activities like painting, crafting, or playing music channels your energy into something positive and restorative.

Practice gratitude by taking a moment each day to reflect on something that went well or something you're thankful for, even if it's a small victory. Celebrate students making progress or having a productive day.

Recognize your limits and take a break; it's okay to recognize when you need a moment to step back and regroup. If you're feeling particularly overwhelmed by a student's behavior, take a brief pause to collect your thoughts or ask for help from a colleague. For example, you might arrange with another teacher or aide to step into your classroom for a few minutes while you take a break. Allowing yourself space to reset can prevent emotional escalation and ensure you're better prepared to re-engage.

Remember to celebrate your successes, no matter how small they may seem. Whether it's a breakthrough with a student, a peaceful transition between activities, or simply making it through a tough day, acknowledging your accomplishments helps you stay motivated. Reflect on these moments and remind yourself of the positive impact you're making, even during challenging times.

Utilize available school resources; many schools offer support for teachers' mental health, such as counseling services or professional development sessions focused on stress management. Take advantage of those opportunities whenever they're available. They can provide you with new coping strategies and help you build a strong support network within your school community.

Teaching is a marathon, not a sprint. Remember, this is a long-term journey. Taking care of your mental health and overall well-being is essential to sustaining your energy and passion for the profession. By practicing self-care, seeking support, and using tools to manage stress, you're not only helping yourself but also modeling healthy habits for your students. When teachers take care of themselves, they're better equipped to create a positive and nurturing classroom environment.

Use the following checklist to commit to weekly self-care management.

The following is a list of things you can do to care for yourself.

SELF-CARE CHECKLIST

Self-care isn't an act but a loving commitment to oneself. How did you cherish yourself this week? At the end of the week it's time for yourself pick at least two things from this list to do for yourself.

- ☐ Take a long bath
- ☐ Engage in a hobby
- ☐ Read for pleasure
- ☐ Listen to your favorite music
- ☐ Go for a long walk
- ☐ Spend time with a loved one
- ☐ Practice mindful meditation
- ☐ Watch a light-hearted movie
- ☐ Journal your thoughts
- ☐ Pamper yourself
- ☐ Try gentle yoga
- ☐ Take a short nap
- ☐ Cook a nourishing meal
- ☐ Go for a swim
- ☐ Visit a museum or gallery
- ☐ Practice gratitude
- ☐ Gardening
- ☐ Attend a workshop or class
- ☐ Paint or draw
- ☐ Explore a new place

Figure 17 Self-Care Checklist Example

True Trigger Tales: Anecdotes from Ms. Alana

Below are examples from my own experience where I identified student triggers and handled the situations with sensitivity, patience, and humor.

****

I gave another behavior therapist (BT) a break and walked into the classroom to find crayons and markers scattered all over the floor and table. I asked the BT what happened. She replied, "We were just sitting here, and he got mad and threw the markers. I told him to clean up, and he threw the rest of the markers and crayons."

I responded. "Well, I guess I won't ask him to clean up then," and the child laughed.

I asked him if he wanted to talk, and he shook his head no.

I asked if he could draw instead, and he said yes. He drew three people, one of whom was big. I asked who the big person was, and he pointed to me.

I joked, "Boy, don't put me in your mess! I wasn't even here. Don't try to get me caught up."

He laughed. I then asked if the other character was the other BT, and he said yes. I asked about the other people in the drawing, and he said it was him and the kid sitting next to him.

I said, "Oh, so the BT wasn't paying any attention to you and was giving the other kid attention, and you didn't like it, so you threw the stuff on the floor?"

He said yes. I continued, "And then she asked you to clean up, and you didn't like that either?"

He said no, he didn't. Throughout our conversation, I pointed to the crayons and markers and then to the bin, and he put them back where they belonged.

I discovered the initial trigger was his need for attention from the BT, and the second trigger was being told to clean up. While gathering this information, I also managed to get him to clean up just by pointing to what I wanted him to do.

****

The student shut down, stopped working on his math, and walked out of the center. I started walking with him and asked what was wrong, but he didn't respond. I noticed he had drawn all over his arms.

I said, "Oh, look at that work you got on your arms! Who did that masterpiece? Did it hurt?"

He laughed, and I said, "That's some mighty fine scribble-scribble you got there. It's almost as good as mine. Would you like to see?"

He said yes. I told him, "Well, you have to turn around and start walking back to the center."

He agreed, and as we walked back, I showed him one of my tattoos.

I then asked why he walked out of the center in the first place, and he said he was mad because there were too many math problems.

I said, "For each math problem you do, I can show you one of my tattoos." I thought to myself, *"Phew, I'm glad I have a lot of tattoos!"*

I told him we could do half the page now and half the page later, so it didn't seem like as much work. Once he finished the whole page, he was able to pick two temporary tattoos from a pack to put on himself.

I discovered the trigger was too many math problems. I modified his work by breaking the work into halves and completing them at separate times. I got him safely back to the center and incentivized him to complete the work by showing him my tattoos.

****

Driving back to work from lunch, I saw a student walking towards the street with my fellow behavioral therapist following closely behind him.

Recognizing the potential danger, I rolled down my window and firmly told him to stop because it was unsafe. I waited until my colleague caught up to him, parked my car, and then approached to assess the situation.

When I spoke to the student, he began pacing back and forth. My partner and I quickly noticed a pattern: as he paced, he wouldn't move past her if she stepped forward. We used this observation to guide him, step by step, back onto campus and toward the library. While I continued to engage with him, my partner discreetly texted for additional support.

As we walked, I encouraged him to share what was bothering him.

Eventually, he opened up and told me he was upset because his group hadn't let him write on the poster as he wanted, and in frustration, he had ripped it. This small but meaningful breakthrough helped us understand his behavior and begin addressing the root cause of his distress.

To de-escalate the situation further, the school psychologist offered her office as a safe space for him to work on a new poster. I encouraged him to visit the supply room to pick out a replacement poster. After some gentle persuasion, he agreed.

We then gave him the choice of working in either the psychologist's office or the speech therapist's office. He chose the psychologist's office, which gave him some sense of control and security.

This experience reinforced the importance of teamwork, patience, and time when managing challenging behaviors. Although the student wasn't part of our program, we were able to quickly build a rapport with him, keep him safe, and help him express what was wrong.

No matter how difficult a situation may seem, you are not alone.

Collaboration and communication with your team makes a

significant difference. Never hesitate to ask for help- it's often the key to resolving even the most challenging scenarios.

****

A student shut down during math and refused to work. He put his head on the table and wouldn't respond, no matter how much I tried to talk to him. I encouraged him gently by asking him to use thumbs up and thumbs down, but he stayed quiet.

Realizing I needed to shift my approach, I decided to focus on creating an engaging environment around him. I started working with other students in the room, making the lesson fun and interactive. I cheered them on with enthusiasm. "Oh yeah, shake those dice and roll 'em!"

I moved to the next student, saying, "Okay, I see you. Let's see what we've got over here!"

As I made my way around the room, keeping the energy light and encouraging, I noticed the student slowly lift his head and begin writing on his paper.

The moment I saw him engage, I ran over to him with excitement, praising him for his effort. "Look at you working! That's what I'm talking about!"

I hyped him up, giving him the positive attention he needed, and he responded by continuing to work. He had his very own hype woman until he finished his work. This is to remind you of the importance of flexibility in behavior management and teaching. When one strategy doesn't work, it doesn't mean it's a failure-it just might not be the right fit for that moment. The key is to quickly assess the situation, adjust your approach, and try something new.

Creating a positive atmosphere and celebrating small steps encourages students to re-engage on their own terms. Success in the classroom isn't about sticking rigidly to one plan; it's about adapting to meet the needs of your students in real time.

Conclusion:
The Final Steps to Behavioral Success

As we wrap up this guide, remember your role as a teacher extends far beyond delivering lessons or managing academic progress. You are a guide, mentor, and supporter of every student's social-emotional growth. The strategies shared here are not one-size-fits-all solutions but tools to help you meet your students where they are. By understanding their triggers, implementing proactive strategies, and fostering meaningful relationships, you are creating a foundation for success that reaches far beyond the classroom.

Using behavior strategies requires patience, empathy, and a willingness to learn from your experiences. Not every strategy will work the first time, and error allows you to better understand what each student needs to thrive. Celebrate small victories; don't be discouraged by setbacks. Each step forward is progress; each effort you make leaves a lasting impression on your students.

It's also important to recognize you are not alone in this work.

Collaboration is key to managing behaviors effectively. Strong relationships with colleagues, behaviorists, and other specialists let you tap into a wealth of knowledge and support. This network of resources helps you develop effective strategies while reminding you that you are part of a larger community dedicated to student success.

One of the most valuable lessons in behavior management is prevention is always better than reaction. Creating predictable routines, teaching functional communication, and using proactive strategies like priming and token boards can significantly reduce challenging behaviors. Clear expectations and reinforcing positive actions create an environment where students feel safe, supported, and motivated to succeed.

Another takeaway is the importance of reflection and adaptability.

Each class and each student presents a unique set of challenges and opportunities. Reflect on what works, adjust what doesn't, and remain flexible in your approach.

By staying open to change and embracing growth, you set an example for your students to do the same.

As much as this book focuses on supporting students, it's equally important to support yourself. Teaching is a demanding job, and managing behavior can be especially taxing. Practicing self-care, seeking help when needed, and setting boundaries are essential for maintaining your well-being. When you prioritize your mental and emotional health, you are better equipped to handle challenges and create a positive environment for your students.

Teaching behavior strategies is about building relationships and helping students develop the skills they need to navigate the world. These are life skills that extend far beyond the classroom and impact their ability to succeed in future academic, social, and professional settings. Your work makes a difference- not just for the moment, but for a lifetime.

As you continue your teaching journey, trust your instincts, use the strategies you've learned, and never underestimate the power of kindness and connection. A simple act of empathy, a moment of patience, or a word of encouragement can transform the trajectory of a student's day, even their life.

This book is not an endpoint but a stepping stone. Continue to seek out new strategies, share your experiences with others, and remain a lifelong learner. The more you grow, the more you help your students do the same.

Thank you for the time, energy, and heart you dedicate to your students.

The work you do matters immensely, and your efforts to create a supportive and inclusive classroom shape the next generation. Keep striving, keep learning, and keep believing in the potential of every student. Together, we can create classrooms where every child feels valued, understood, and empowered to succeed.

Resources

The following pages include all the tracking sheets and visuals referenced throughout the book, provided here for you to easily make copies as needed. If there are any sheets you'd like a clearer version of, feel free to email me, and I'll be happy to send you the specific page you need.

spectrumprotection2@gmail.com

If you are interested in scheduling a teacher training session at your school, please visit spectrumprotectionllc.com and contact me for availability and booking.

TRIGGER TRACKER

MONTH : _____

STRATEGY	1	2	3	4	5	6	7	8	9	10	11	12	13	14	15	16	17	18	19	20	21	22	23	24	25	26	27	28	29	30	31
SMELLS																															
TRANSITIONS																															
LOUD NOISES																															
HUNGER																															
LACK OF SLEEP																															
BRIGHT LIGHTS																															
PHYSICAL ILLNESS																															
ACADEMICS																															
CLOTHING TEXTURES																															
PEER CONFLICT																															
TEMPATURE																															
CONGITIVE OVERLOAD																															
FIRE ALARM																															
CROWDED ENVIRONMENT																															
SUBSTITUTE TEACHERS																															
OTHER																															

NOTES

RESULTS

TRIGGER TRACKER

Date:

Start Time:

Finish Time:

Duration:

Location:

Possible Triggers:
Loud noises   Bright lights   Strong smells   Crowded environment   Hunger
Lack of sleep   Physical illness   Academics   Transitioning between activities
Temperature   Clothing texture   Cognitive overload   Peer conflict   Fire alarm
Substitute teachers

If not here add it:

What subject was going:

What actions were taken:

What Happened:

Strategies used:

SELF-CARE CHECKLIST

Self-care isn't an act but a loving commitment to oneself. How did you cherish yourself this week? At the end of the week it's time for yourself pick at least two things from this list to do for yourself.

- [ ] Take a long bath
- [ ] Read for pleasure
- [ ] Go for a long walk
- [ ] Practice mindful meditation
- [ ] Journal your thoughts
- [ ] Try gentle yoga
- [ ] Cook a nourishing meal
- [ ] Visit a museum or gallery
- [ ] Gardening
- [ ] Paint or draw

- [ ] Engage in a hobby
- [ ] Listen to your favorite music
- [ ] Spend time with a loved one
- [ ] Watch a light-hearted movie
- [ ] Pamper yourself
- [ ] Take a short nap
- [ ] Go for a swim
- [ ] Practice gratitude
- [ ] Attend a workshop or class
- [ ] Explore a new place

FINISH

ALL DONE

HELP

SPACE

OUR DAILY
CLASS SCHEDULE

8:50am	Writing
9:35am	Special
10:20am	Recess
11:05am	Art
11:50am	Lunch
12:35pm	Math
1:20pm	Science
2:05pm	Science/Social Studies

Weekly schedule

	Monday	Tuesday	Wednesday	Thursday	Friday
08:30	Morning Meeting	Morning Meeting	Morning Meeting	Morning Meeting	Assembly
09:00	Music	Reading	Reading	Reading	Reading
9:30	Therapy	Writing	Writing	Writing	Therapy
10:00	Recess	Recess	Recess	Recess	Recess
10:30	Speech	Art	Art	Art	Art
11:00	Library	PE	Library	PE	Music
11:30	Math	Math	Math	Math	Math
12:00	Lunch	Lunch	Lunch	Lunch	Lunch
12:30	Science	Science	Science	Science	Science

Note:

medication tracker.

medication	dose	start	stop	side effects

Token Board

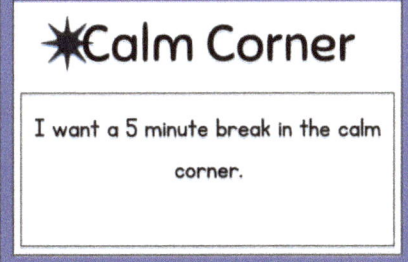

CALM DOWN CHART

take a nap

drink water

draw

jump

watch a funny video

stretch

kick a ball

read a book

sing a song

snack break

meditation

play with a fidgets

STRATEGY TRACKER

MONTH: _____

Habit	1	2	3	4	5	6	7	8	9	10	11	12	13	14	15	16	17	18	19	20	21	22	23	24	25	26	27	28	29	30	31	Result
Use Timers																																
Visual Supports																																
Snacks (eating)																																
First/Then Board																																
Offer Breaks																																
Choices																																
Sensory accommodations																																
Breathing Exercises																																
Environmental Modifications																																
Priming																																
Break Task Into Smaller Steps																																
Notes:																																

FIRST/THEN BOARD

First   **Then**

CALMING STRATEGIES

weighted blankets	create a calm corner
fidgets	music
blow bubbles	take a break (have a snack, read, be alone)
yell into a pillow	rip paper or boxes
break popsicle sticks	go for a walk
pressure massage (head, arms, legs)	headphones, earplugs
give space (set a timer and check-in)	drawing
deep breathing	drink water
make a fort	squeeze playdough or clay
chewing gum	kinetic sand
play with slime	run a lap
legos	stress ball

PRIMING STRATEGIES

establish a routine	use visual supports
use timers	break tasks into smaller steps
relaxation techniques	calm and self-regulation techniques
social stories	choices
positive reinforcement	muscle relaxation
environmental modifications	breathing exercises
praise	sensory accommodations
first/then strategies	provide supportive guidance
offer breaks	be consistent
model expected behavior	use positive language to frame the task
make it fun	set clear expectations

DISRUPTION TRACKER

MONTH : _____

DISRUPTIVE BEHAVIOR	1	2	3	4	5	6	7	8	9	10	11	12	13	14	15	16	17	18	19	20	21	22	23	24	25	26	27	28	29	30	31
BLURT OUTS																															
SHUT DOWN																															
INAPPROPRIATE LANGUAGE																															
OFF TASK																															
DISRESPECTFUL																															
DISTRACTING OTHERS																															
ARGUING																															
AGGRESSION																															
THROWING OBJECTS																															
WANDERING ROOM																															
INAPPROPRIATE NOISES																															
EMOTIONAL OUTBURST																															
ELOPING																															
INAPPROPRIATE USE OF COMPUTER																															
YELLING																															
REFUSING INSTRUCTION																															

ANTECEDENT   RESULTS

_____   _____
_____   _____
_____   _____
_____   _____
_____   _____

www.ingramcontent.com/pod-product-compliance
Lightning Source LLC
Chambersburg PA
CBHW061234070526
44584CB00030B/4114